EIGHTEEN

6/10/71

The Poetry of John G. Hunter III

Compiled by
Bradford G. Wheler

EIGHTEEN
6/10/71

The Poetry of John G. Hunter III

Compiled by Bradford G. Wheler

BookCollaborative.com
PO box 403
Cazenovia, NY 13035
Editor@www.BookCollaborative.com

ISBN-13   978-0-9822538-1-6

Library of Congress Control Number: 2009910550
poetry

PRINTER IN THE UNITED STATES OF AMERICA

Cover design by AuthorSupport.com
Interior design by Adina Cucicov, Flamingo Designs

Introduction

It has been my pleasure to known John Hunter since I was about 5 years old. The poetry in this book, was given to me by John, as my eighteenth birthday present on 6/10/71. It was a hand written collection of 18 poems John had written sometime before June of 1971. John is one year older so all these poems were written before John was nineteen.

I'm sure I received many fine gifts for my eighteenth birthday but this is the only one I still have and treasure.

Those of you who know John already know all that I am about to say. John is a wonderful and unique friend. He has a wide range of friends literally all around the world. He is an adventurer who has climbed Mount Everest several times breaking the 20,000 ft. mark. He has climbed mountains, skied, and trekked in Europe, Africa, Asia, North America, and South America. John is a gifted athlete who makes skiing, golf and tennis look easy.

John has taken me on many of his less strenuous adventures. Several times rescuing me from near death experiences. Saving him the embarrassment of explaining what happened to my mother.

John spent over a dozen years living in Dubai. He studied in Italy for two years and holds a BS from Loyola University in Chicago and a Masters Degree in international management from the Thunderbird School of Global Management in Arizona.

I'm not sure how many other volumes of poetry John has written but my hope is you will enjoy this one. I've enjoyed it for over 38 years since I received it on June 10, 1971.

Bradford G. Wheler
Cazenovia, New York
December 2009

Life is hard, hard as love
Hard as the death of a puppy
To a little girl
Life is as hard as the sea
On a stormy nite
As hard as the ever present unknown
As hard as the longest wait
Life is as hard as the soft last kiss
Life is hard, hard as the joy of love
Life is hard, as hard as I make it

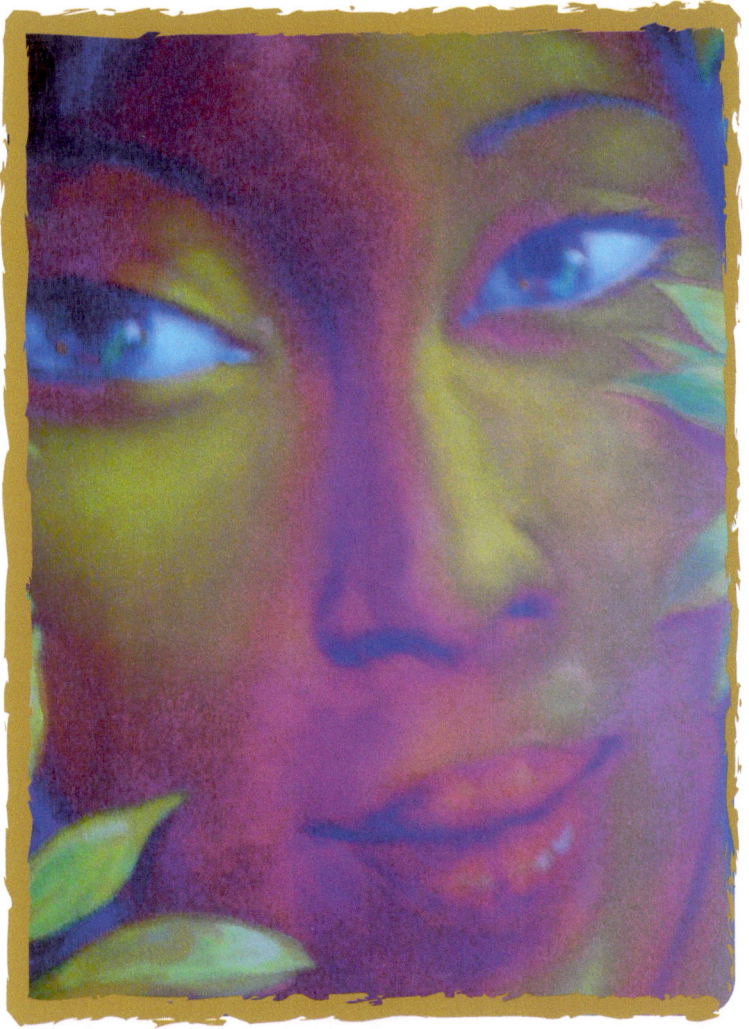

Don't believe me
When I say you are
Wonderful—
But look in yourself
And say it to me
Then believe it
And you will have something
To love

Yesterday is not for worry
Today.
Today is for you to think
Of tomorrow.

Its probably not sunny
Where you are
For last time I saw you
Your eyes never glistened
As they stared at the fire
Seeking answers—
And your lips never smiled

So it all so bad
That you can't free yourself
And run with me for a
Brief time—
Don't watch the fire for answers

Yesterday is gone
Tomorrow not yet here –
Time in between is mysterious
And waiting.
Its these moments when
Time is quiet
And we are at peace
With him.
Time looks at me
Then you, smiles abound
Parting kisses, and time and I
Leave
To find my golden moments
Between yesterday and tomorrow

Searching for the sun
Following the wind
Wanting things clear and bright –
But I've learned the most
Talking to the fog

Where am I headed you ask—
Much like the wind I don't know
Much like the wind I'm free—
The wind goes and searches
And still knows not
Where its going for when it gets there
It will stop

The wind has been moving
A long time and its still searching
And I who was just born, how can
You expect an answer from me

To know love is beautiful
But remember she will come
Briefly now and then
Until she is ready to come and stay

Problems lead to appreciation
Appreciation to love
Love to life—

To turn to others
When you are not sure
Is not always the answer—
For they are not sure what
You are

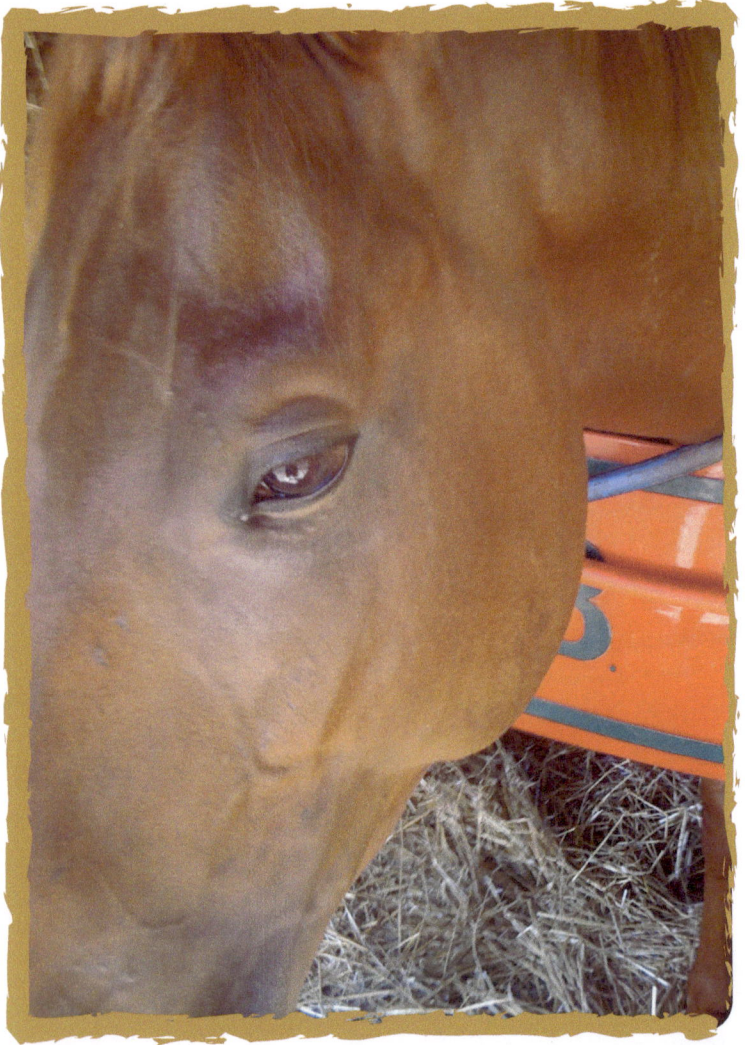

If you can't live
With something
And you can't live
Without it
You just have to leave it behind

For a while

Then to return the same,
And yet new—
To start with the old
Over again
To be yourself

The far side of the hill
I've been there, and you
Ask me to go again—
Well, I loved it there
And if I took you
You would only see it
As I saw it—
Go by yourself and
For yourself, you'll
Return better.
One thing I do ask
When you're on top of the hill
And before you plunge down
The far side
Stop—and look at both sides.

Once on coming home
I stopped to think of where I was
Finding no answer, I turned
And still I follow the wind
I only hope the wind
Is smarter than I

Once in a dark chamber
I sat, watching an ember die.
Suddenly, from I know not where, came
A voice so sweet I had to smile.
I saw no face, I felt no body,
Only a voice of spring.
I spoke, but stopped, for it vanished.
Now often I return, to find nothing
"Life is more than memories" was the last said

If time should ask
Tell him I've gone
Into silence.
Silence soon becomes
Nothing, and nothing becomes
Forever
So tell him love endures
Beyond time—

A memory does not fade
Like a picture.
Which as it fades—
Is forgotten.
But rather a memory soon forgets
The bad and becomes more beautiful
So when I meet her again
I'll love her more

What does it mean for me to tell you
If you don't want to hear it

What does it mean to tell me
If it isn't true

What does it mean to tell the wind
If you can't tell the person

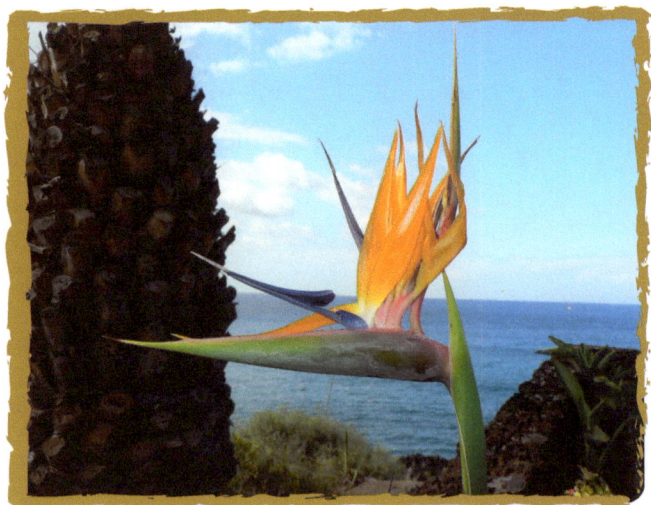

Its only life
That you must love
And accept
To find and hold
One small thing
And call it yourself
To accept and build with
That one small thing—
Its very hard to hold
One grain of sand
But never let go
Until it has grown into
Something easy to hold.

About the Author

Bradford G. Wheler is the former CEO, President and Co-owner of Allan Electric Company. He sold the company to a New York Stock Exchange list utility company back when the stock market was hot. Brad retired after staying on as President during a transition period.

Brad's life long love of history, art, books and the humor in man's nature lead to the founding of BookCollaborative.com. as well as the publishing of this book and SNAPPY SAYINGS; wit & wisdom from the world's greatest minds.

His community involvements include being a Trustee of Cazenovia College, A member of the Board of Directors of the Greater Cazenovia Area Chamber of Commerce, and Chairman of the Board of Directors and Alumni Association President of Sigma Phi Society at Cornell University in Ithaca, NY.

Brad hold's a BS and ME in Civil and Environmental Engineering from Cornell University in Ithaca, NY. He has a MBA degree from Fordham University in New York, NY and is a Licensed Professional Engineer in New York and several other states. He is also a graduate of the Manlius Pebble Hill School.

Brad lives with his wife Julie and their golden retriever Quincy in Cazenovia, NY.

Buy These Books

"EIGHTEEN 6/10/71 The Poetry Of John G. Hunter III"
and "SNAPPY SAYINGS; wit & wisdom from the world's
greatest minds" are available on
Amazom.com and Barns&Noble.com.
You can also order them at any bookstore in the US, UK,
and Canada for delivery within a few days.